AIRPORT SECURITY WITH NOONORSE

Author and Illustrator: Diana Lipnick-Feld

Published by feld studios, Los Angeles, CA.
www.feldstudios.com | @dianalipnickfeld

Global distribution by IngramSpark | Available on Amazon.com
Text and Illustrations copyright © 2019 Diana Lipnick-Feld
Library of Congress Control Number: 2019912353
New Edition, 2019

Publisher's Cataloging-In-Publication Data
(Prepared by The Donohue Group, Inc.)

Names: Lipnick-Feld, Diana, author, illustrator.
Title: Airport security with Noonorse / by Diana Lipnick-Feld.
Description: [New edition]. | Los Angeles, CA : Feld Studio, [2019] | "For Maya and Theo Klein."| Includes game recognition pages that decode airport symbols and a vocabulary of common terms associated with air travel. | Interest age level: 002-005. | Summary: "Noonorse is a fluffy, cuddly bear that will accompany children, ages two to five, on their flight adventures and help them understand the sequence of what happens before boarding a plane, from checking bags to going through security to showing the flight attendant their boarding pass. It also teaches young children the symbols that can be found in airports"--Provided by publisher.
Identifiers: ISBN 9780999653722 (paperback) | ISBN 9780999653715 (hardback) | ISBN 9780999653739 (ebook)
Subjects: LCSH: Bears--Juvenile fiction. | Air travel--Juvenile fiction. | Airports--Juvenile fiction. | Airline passenger security screening--Juvenile fiction. | CYAC: Bears--Fiction. | Air travel--Fiction. | Airports--Fiction.
Classification: LCC PZ7.1.L566 Ai 2019 (print) | LCC PZ7.1.L566 (ebook) | DDC [E]--dc23

I am grateful to the following contributors to this book:
First, thank you to all the teddy bears, all over the world, for sharing childhood with us; and to Maya and Theo Klein, whose playfulness, love, enthusiasm, and generosity have inspired this project;

Copy Editors: Amanda Klein and Athena Gam
Storyboard Artist: Terrence McFarden
Life Drawing Models: Athena Gam and Pamela Debiase
Graphic Design: Tara Feld, www.tarafelddesign.com, @tarafelddesign
Web Design and Development: Kathy Moran, www.webdevelopmentartistry.com
Book Sherpa: Gail M. Kearns, To Press & Beyond, www.topressandbeyond.com
Ebook Conversion & Distribution: ebookPartnership team, www.ebook.partnership.com
Support Team: Shelly Corwin Dale, Carolyn Kreisman, Jonathan Klein, Eric Lake, and Abe Fuks.
Author Photograph Mural Artist: Ruben Rojas, www.rubenrojas.com
Author Photograph: Tara Feld

Printed in the United States of America

AIRPORT SECURITY WITH NOONORSE

For Maya and Theo Klein

By Diana Lipnick-Feld

Mommy is taking me
on an airplane trip.
I'm so excited
to see my friends
Maya and Theo!

It's my first time
at the airport.
What will I see
when we go inside?

The ticket agent
helps us check in our bag
and gives Mommy
our boarding passes.

At the security checkpoint, everyone takes off their shoes and belts.

We gather our things
so we can head to
the departure gate.

I put my backpack into the bin
with Mommy's shoes.
"Good job!,"
says the TSA agent.

There goes
my backpack,
to get scanned
in the machine!

The TSA Agent tells me it's my turn to go through the metal detector.

I get checked with
a metal detector wand.

I'm too young to go
through the scanner,
but I watch as
Mommy goes through.

Hip hip hooray!
My backpack is here!

Look out the window!
The plane is waiting for us.

It's our turn to board.
I get to show the
flight attendant
our boarding passes.

Our plane is just around the corner.
I can't wait to get on!

I ask to see the cockpit
and the captain says hello.
There are so many buttons,
switches and dials!

All of us passengers
find our seats.
My backpack goes up
in the overhead bin.

Buckle up, Mommy!
Buckle up Noonorse!
CLICK goes the seat belt,
before the plane
goes in the air.

We watch the
safety demonstration,
and then up,
up, up we go!

As we soar through the clouds,
I eat a yummy lunch.
Flying is fun!

I've got to go potty.
Look, here's the toilet.

The water is blue
and the flush is loud…
Whoosh!

Down from the sky we come
and the plane touches down.
The plane has finally landed
and we're back down
on the ground.

As we wait
at the baggage claim,
I'm excited for hugs.
There on the carousel,
our suitcase finally comes.

Wow!
It's my first time seeing
an airport security dog.

Hurry Mommy, let's go.
Maya and Theo
are waiting!

I see pictures of me
and my friends'
smiling faces!

I'm grateful
for this journey
and the love
of my friends.

VOCABULARY AT THE AIRPORT

Below are some words you can learn that describe what you might find or experience at the airport. Flip through the pictures of this book and name some of the things you see.

airplane, ascending, baggage cart, flying, take-off, lift-off

airport terminal, departures, entrance, passenger drop-off area, taxi

baggage, carry-on bag, luggage, suitcase, backpack, purse

airline ticket agent, baggage check-in area, boarding pass, ticket

airport security area, baggage and passenger scanning, bin

walk-in scanner

TSA agent, metal detector wand

flight attendant, boarding pass, gate, passenger waiting area

VOCABULARY AT THE AIRPORT

Here are some more words you can learn that describe the people, places and things that you might find at the airport and on an airplane. A fun way to learn the meaning of these words is to look through the pages of this book with a friend, point at the pictures, and name some of the things that you see out loud.

boarding line-up area, airplane entrance, ramp

captain, co-pilot, cockpit, flight crew, safety demonstration

fasten seat belts, in-flight safety card, beverages, snacks, meal

landing, ground crew, runway, unfasten seat belts

baggage claim area, baggage carousel

security dog, dog vest, airport security officer

airport passenger arrival area, airport terminal exit

transportation area, taxi area, bus stop, shuttle buses

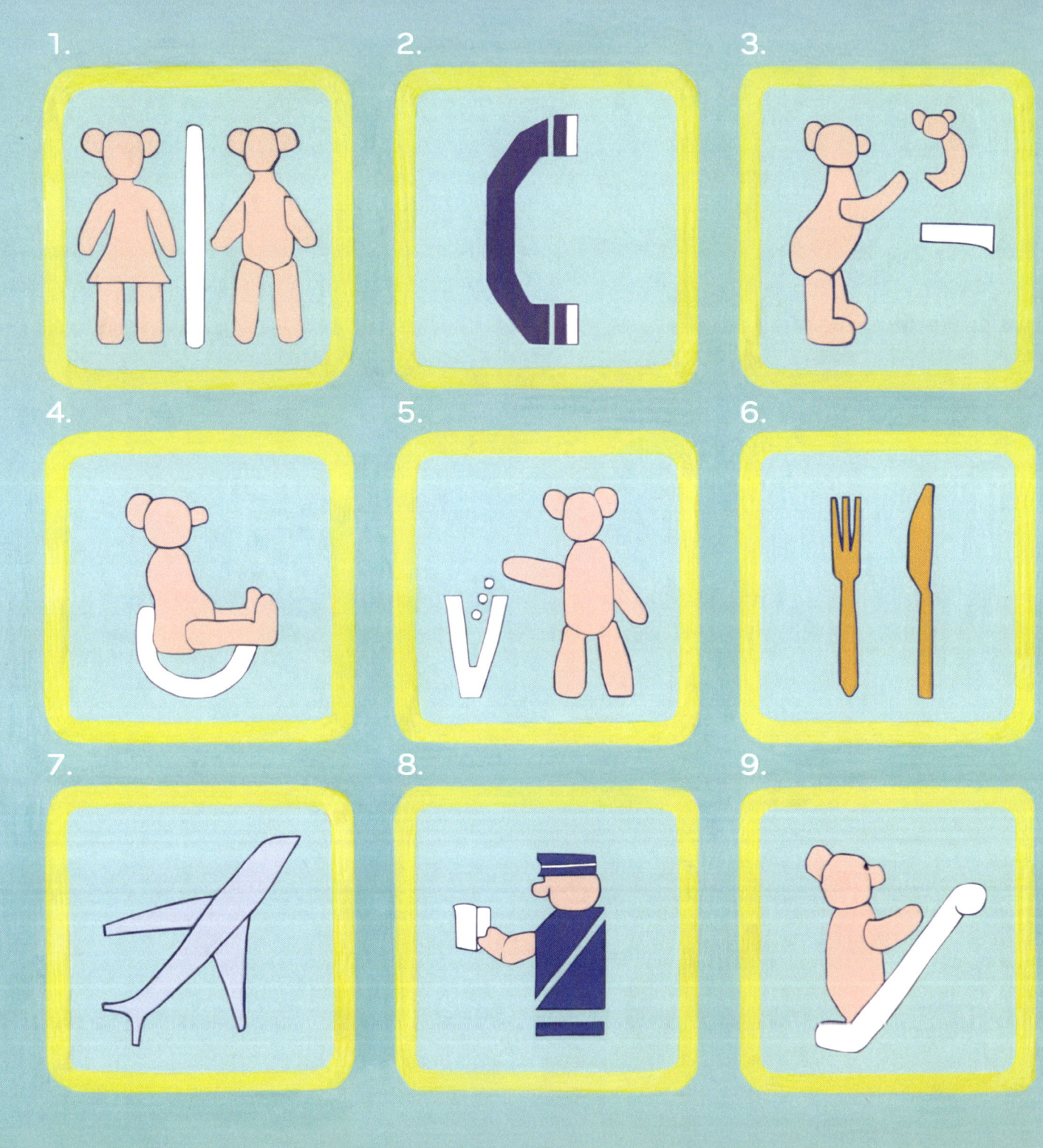

DECODING AIRPORT SYMBOLS

Here are some signs similar to those that you might see at the airport. Play a game by decoding the symbols on each sign. Try to match the picture on the GREEN page with the corresponding sign name on the opposite page.

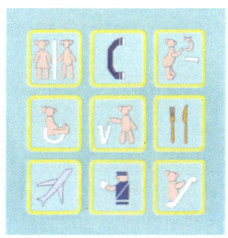

Green Page Sign Names

Baby Care
Escalator
Flight Departures
Immigration
Litter Disposal/ Trash Can
Restaurant
Telephone
Toilets
Wheelchair Accessible

Answer Key: 1. Toilets, 2. Telephone, 3. Baby Care, 4. Wheelchair Accessible, 5. Litter Disposal/ Trash Can, 6. Restaurant, 7. Flight Departures, 8. Immigration, 9. Escalator.

Decoding Questions:

Point to the sign that tells you where you can throw something away.

Which sign would you look for if you had to "go potty", or go to the bathroom?

Point to which symbol would help you find a place where can you can go to eat a meal.

What sign would you follow to help you find a way to get upstairs?

Answer Key: 5. Litter Disposal/ Trash Can, 1. Toilets, 6. Restaurant, 9. Escalator.

DECODING AIRPORT SYMBOLS

Here are some signs similar to those that you might see at the airport. Play a game by decoding the symbols on each sign. Try to match the picture on the PINK page with the corresponding sign name on the right.

Pink Page Sign Names

Air Transportation
Arriving Flights
Baggage Carts
Bus
Coffee Shop
Customs
Drinking Fountain
Elevator
Transfer

Answer Key: 1. Baggage Carts, 2. Coffee Shop, 3. Elevator, 4. Transfer, 5. Drinking Fountain, 6. Bus, 7. Air Transportation, 8. Customs, 9. Arriving Flights.

Decoding Questions:

What sign should you look for if you are feeling thirsty and need a drink of water?

What sign will help you find a way to go up or down to a different floor level at the airport?

Is there a sign that you can point to that would help you find a drink or a snack to eat?

Point to the sign that you would follow to take a ride to somewhere you want to go?

Answer Key: 5. Drinking Fountain, 3. Elevator, 2. Coffee Shop, 6. Bus.

DECODING AIRPORT SYMBOLS

Here are some signs similar to those that you might see at the airport. Play a game by decoding the symbols on each sign. Try to match the picture on the PURPLE page with the corresponding sign name on the right.

Purple Page Sign Names

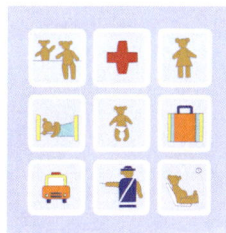

Baggage Check-In
First Aid
Hotel
Nursery
Policeman
Taxi
Ticket Purchase/ Agent
Waiting Room
Women's Toilet

Answer Key: 1. Ticket Purchase/ Agent, 2. First Aid, 3. Women's Toilet, 4. Hotel, 5. Nursery, 6. Baggage Check-In, 7. Taxi, 8. Policeman, 9. Waiting Room.

Decoding Questions:

What sign shows you where you can pick up your boarding passes for your flight?

Is there a sign that you can point to that would help you to know where to check in a suitcase for the flight?

Point to the symbol you would find on a sign where you could get help if you needed a band aid?

What sign shows you a picture of who to ask for help if you get lost or separated from your family?

Answer Key: 1. Ticket Purchase/ Agent, 6. Baggage Check-in, 2. First Aid, 8. Policeman.

ABOUT THE AUTHOR

Author Photograph © Tara Feld

Diana Lipnick-Feld is an artist living in Los Angeles. Inspired by everyday life and nature, she delights in telling stories through her bookmaking, collage, painting, and sculpture.

Noonorse the bear, a gift from Diana's parents to their great-grandchildren, became her companion on a transcontinental flight from France to the United States. Noonorse is the transliteration of "Nounours", the French word for bear.

On her journey with Noonorse, Diana had to show the bear for scanning at every security checkpoint. During many hours lined-up at the airport and waiting to board airplanes, Diana began to sketch her surroundings.

One drawing lead to another and the story of a traveling bear, excited to be united with the children who love him was born.

www.ingramcontent.com/pod-product-compliance
Lightning Source LLC
Chambersburg PA
CBRC090838010526
44118CB00008B/248